The CYA Guide to Payroll and HR

Christina Hageny,
CPP, PHR, SHRM-CP

www.TotalPublishingAndMedia.com

ISBN: 978-1-63302-243-0

Dedication

This book is dedicated to all the entrepreneurs working to build their dreams.

"Books are the training weights
of the mind."

— Epictetus

Table of Contents

Why Read This Book?

You started your business because you loved your craft. You are passionate about what you do, and confident customers want what you're offering. Yet the dream of owning your own business can quickly become a nightmare if you don't take responsibilities of an employer seriously.

If you're thinking "But I do care, I just don't have time", you are not alone. But where do you start? Although it may sound cliché, you don't know what you don't know. If you're not familiar with the core principles of payroll and how laws can differ from one state to another, there's no possible way you can set up and process payroll with 100% accuracy and compliance.

A common fallacy with new-age payroll technology is that payroll is somehow easier if we have access to a system with simple menus and big buttons. However, end users of popular products like QuickBooks and Gusto have become quickly and painfully aware that payroll compliance requires knowledge and skills novice payroll processors do not possess – penalties and interest stack up just as fast as notices from federal and state agencies.

Maybe, just maybe, if we gave business owners a quick overview of the basics, we can help them eliminate or prevent the vast majority of mistakes they might otherwise make.

We created this guide to be a 10,000 foot view of payroll and HR compliance, designed to cover the basics and provide direct links to additional resources.

It doesn't have to be this hard!

Acknowledgements

First and foremost, I would like to thank my husband, Rusty, for encouraging me to start the amazing journey of entrepreneurship. Without him I never would have taken this leap, and without his constant support I could not have accomplished this dream. Thank you, babe.

I would also like to thank my parents for always pushing me to go beyond the limits of what I thought was possible. From birth they have instilled in me an "old-school" work ethic, and taught me that mediocrity and complacency are never acceptable.

Foreword

After working with hundreds of small business owners, the major pitfalls these entrepreneurs experience have become abundantly clear. Although the number of issues related to payroll and HR are extensive, I know if business owners educated themselves on the major compliance pieces of running a business, they can significantly reduce their liability – which is why we have created this guide.

I have personally witnessed small businesses migrating away from "big box" payroll companies and the DIY platforms to work with small, "locally owned" payroll solutions. I didn't understand what was causing them to leave in droves. This all changed when I started my payroll practice in 2020. With zero clients (and zero income) I began seeking jobs on UpWork. I was surprised to find the same companies who chose the absolute cheapest payroll solution also opted to pay my premium hourly consulting rate, for assistance with various payroll tasks. The math didn't add up for me.

With so many DIY platforms like Gusto and QuickBooks, businesses are enticed to do payroll in-house. These online software programs have visually appealing user interfaces and large buttons designed to make payroll "easy". In effect, these products have removed the guardrails necessary to keep your payroll car from catapulting off a very steep cliff. Easy to click buttons do not equate to sound payroll practices. The user of the software should be knowledgeable about federal, state, and sometimes local rules and regulations, which are endless and constantly changing.

I was grateful for the opportunity to be paid to wait on hold with the IRS or QuickBooks support, but at the end of the day I also support small businesses and found it a disservice that there was no quick guide available for business owners who were getting ready to hire their first employee. I'm happy to watch DIY fails on Pinterest projects, but couldn't stomach another small business owner trying to do right and coming up short when it comes to payroll and HR.

This is why I set out to create this guide. As a small business owner, I truly have a passion for helping small business owners and entrepreneurs succeed. I hope this tool empowers employers to understand the basics of payroll and HR, and apply best practices within their company.

Employee or Contractor?

It is your obligation to <u>classify</u> your worker properly. This does not mean you choose whether you want to give the worker a 1099 or a W-2! According to the IRS[1], "the general rule[2] is that an individual is an independent contractor if the payer has the right to control or direct only the result of the work, not *what and how* it will be done."

---

[1] https://www.irs.gov/newsroom/
understanding-employee-vs-contractor-designation

[2] https://www.irs.gov/newsroom/
employee-or-independent-contractor-know-the-rules

Your worker is most likely an employee if you:

- Set the schedule (when work will stop, start, and when breaks can be taken)
- Provide the tools required to perform the work
- Provide any training on how the work will be performed
- Offer him/her benefits

Your worker is most likely an independent contractor if:

- They offer services to other clients in addition to you
- They have the potential for loss
- They have unreimbursed expenses
- They provide their own equipment and methods for completing the job

The DOL has a whole webpage to dispel myths about employee v. contractor classification[3].

Here are the most common errors I see:
- Misclassifying a worker as a contractor because they are a temporary employee
- Misclassifying a worker as a contractor because they paid them less than $600 during the year
- Misclassifying a worker as a contractor because they are in a trial or introductory period
- Misclassifying a worker as a contractor because the worker only worked for one hour, day, or shift (very short period of time)

---

[3]   https://www.dol.gov/agencies/whd/flsa/misclassification/myths

Employers may try to reduce payroll costs by knowingly misclassifying employees as independent contractors. With such a long list of additional expenses, it may seem like a no-brainer to classify all your workers as independent contractors.

The expenses of having an employee include:
- Social Security tax – 6.2% up to the annual wage base
- Medicare tax – 1.45% on all taxable wages
- State unemployment tax – The state determines their wage base and assigns the employer an individual unemployment insurance tax rate
- Federal unemployment tax – 6% of the first $7,000 in wages with up to a 5.4% credit
- Workers compensation insurance

- Minimum wage and overtime per FLSA[4] (or state laws if more favorable to the employee)
- Health insurance (if employer is an Applicable Large Employer[5] or ALE)
- Paid family and/or medical leave (depending on state and employer size)

Before making this mistake, employers should also be aware of the consequences of misclassifying an employee as an independent contractor.

---

[4]   https://www.dol.gov/agencies/whd/flsa
[5]   https://www.irs.gov/affordable-care-act/employ-ers/determining-if-an-employer-is-an-applicable-large-employer#:~:text=Two%20provisions%20of%20the%20Affordable,employer%20shared%20responsibility%20provisions%3B%20and

If the IRS determines an employee has been misclassified as an independent contractor, they can penalize the employer with:

- A $50 fine per W-2 that the employer failed to furnish
- 3% of the employee's wages (plus interest)
- Up to 40% of the employee's FICA taxes
- Up to 100% of the employer's FICA taxes
- A Failure to Pay Taxes penalty equal to 0.5% of the unpaid tax liability for each month, up to 25% of the total tax liability.

Employers may also face penalties for failure to pay overtime or minimum wage, unemployment insurance shortfalls, and I-9 violations. The bottom-line is employers cannot afford to misclassify employees!

Exempt or Non-Exempt Employee

According to the Fair Labor Standards Act (FLSA), non-exempt employees are guaranteed a minimum wage of at least $7.25 per hour, and overtime pay (one and a half times the regular rate of pay) for all hours worked over 40 in a workweek. Exempt employees are not guaranteed minimum wage or overtime pay, and therefore it is imperative you correctly classify your employees.

The FLSA is extremely specific on who qualifies as an exempt employee. Only employees whose **duties and salaries** meet the minimum requirements can be considered exempt from minimum wage and overtime provisions. As of 2022, the minimum salary for an exempt employee is $35,568 per year. You can check out the FLSA's Fact Sheet[6] for details on those exemptions. Certain states, such as California, have their own laws about exempt employees, and the employer must always follow whichever laws are more favorable to the employee.

The most common myth I encounter is paying an employee a salary makes them an exempt employee, which is 100% false. An employee's duties must fall into one of the listed exemptions, and he/she must be paid the minimum salary amount in order to qualify. As a general rule, employees engaged in manual labor or who do not

---

[6] https://www.dol.gov/sites/dolgov/files/WHD/legacy/files/fs17a_overview.pdf

have discretion or control over their job are generally non-exempt employees (blue-collar workers, for example).

If you pay a non-exempt employee a salary, you must also keep track of the hours worked to ensure you also pay 1.5 x's their regular rate for all hours worked over 40 in a workweek.

New Hire Forms

Each time an employee is hired, he or she must complete a series of forms to be set up in payroll:

- W-4[7] – The employee completes the federal W-4 form to denote their tax filing status, claim credits, and claim additional jobs or income. This form is used to set up their federal withholding in your payroll system.

- I-9[8] – The employee should not be asked to complete the I-9 prior to being given a job offer but MUST complete the I-9 no later than their date of hire.

---

[7] https://www.irs.gov/pub/irs-pdf/fw4.pdf

[8] https://www.uscis.gov/sites/default/files/document/forms/i-9.pdf

The employee should only complete Section 1 and provide acceptable documents to the employer (see page 4 of the I-9 for a list of acceptable documents). The employer must complete Section 2 to certify the I-9 within three days of the employee's date of hire.

- o Employers who use or are required to use E-Verify must also make copies of the documents provided and retain those copies with the I-9 forms.
- State Tax Withholding Form (if applicable) – States that have income tax will use the federal W-4 form or a state-specific withholding form.
- Direct Deposit Form (if applicable) – We advise clients to require a voided check or screenshot from a bank portal to confirm the information provided

is accurate. This eliminates direct deposits going into the wrong account or being rejected.

- Offer Letter (optional) – Although not required, an offer letter is a clear way to outline the job, pay rate, pay frequency and benefits, and allows the employee or potential employee to acknowledge their acceptance of the terms in writing.
- Background Check Authorization (optional) – If you will be performing a background check on the employee you MUST have prior authorization.
- Additional handouts or notices as required by state. Some states require you to provide employees certain notifications upon hire.

New Hire Reporting

Each time you hire a new employee, the employer is required to report the new hire's information to the state. If you are a multi-state employer, you have two options – report the employee to the state they work in, or report all new hires to a state where you have employees working.

Some states will accept a federal W-4 in lieu of a new hire form, other states require their own specific form to be completed.

The purpose of new hire reporting is to identify employees who have child support orders or other wage garnishments. If an employee has an active order, a copy of this information will be sent to the employer with instructions on how much to withhold and how to remit the payments.

For a more in-depth look at new hire reporting read SHRM's Complying with New-Hire Reporting Requirements Toolkit[9].

---

[9] https://www.shrm.org/resourcesandtools/tools-and-samples/toolkits/pages/complyingwithnew-hirereportin-grequirements.aspx

Minimum Wage

As of 2022, the federal minimum wage is $7.25 per hour, but many states have their own minimum wage requirements, which are more generous than the federal minimum wage. As with any other employment law, the employer should use whichever is more favorable to the employee in instances where the federal and state (or local) regulations differ.

Certain states allow tip-credits, which means the employer can pay the employee less than minimum wage if the employee makes enough in tips for their compensation to equal (at the least) the minimum wage rate.

If the employer is using a tip credit, they must pay additional wages to the employee if their tips plus wages divided by the total number of hours worked is less than the minimum wage (tip-credit makeup).

Exempt employees are not subject to minimum wage requirements, and do not have to track their hours worked.

Rest and Meal Breaks

According to the Department of Labor (DOL)[10], federal law does not require rest or meal breaks, but many states have enacted rest and/or meal break laws. States without their own policies adhere to the federal provisions and do not grant rest or meal breaks. However, certain exceptions can apply at the state level for minors and nursing mothers. Employers in California[11] should thoroughly read and understand the rest and meal break requirements as theirs are (perhaps) the strictest in the country.

---

10   https://www.dol.gov/general/topic/workhours/breaks
11   https://www.dir.ca.gov/dlse/faq_mealperiods.htm

Paid Sick Leave

There is no federal mandate for employers to provide employees with paid sick leave, but each year more states are enacting policies which require employers to provide some type of paid time off. Arizona, California, Colorado, Connecticut, Illinois (local only), Maine, Maryland, Massachusetts, Michigan, Minnesota (local only), Nevada, New Jersey, New Mexico, New York, Oregon, Pennsylvania (local only), Rhode Island, Vermont, Washington, and Washington DC currently have state-specific policies for employers.

Workers Compensation

With the exception of Texas, all US states require employers to carry workers' compensation insurance to cover on the job injuries or illnesses. Workers' compensation coverage should be active on your employees first day of employment

Like many payroll regulations (overtime, meal breaks, income tax, etc), each state has its own workers' compensation requirements and penalties. To see your state's requirements, you can click visit insureon's website[12].

---

[12] https://www.insureon.com/small-business-insurance/ workers-compensation/state-laws

Four states require you to purchase workers' compensation insurance directly from the state instead of from a private insurer – North Dakota, Ohio, Washington, and Wyoming.

Traditionally, workers' compensation premiums were based on payroll estimates. Employers were required to pay a large down payment in addition to monthly premium amounts based on the original estimates. This can be problematic for companies that have large increases or decreases in their employee headcount – as their original payroll estimates may have been much too high or much too low. Employers are required to go through an annual audit with their workers' compensation provider to determine if any additional premiums are owed, or if the client is due a refund once the policy period has ended, and actual payroll dollars can be computed.

However, employers are more frequently opting for pay-as-you-go options where actual payroll dollars are reported each pay period, and the employer is debited accurate premium amounts. This reduces or eliminates any balance or refund due at the annual audit.

Labor Posters

Federal law requires certain notices to be posted in an employee breakroom or other conspicuous location. States also have their own posting requirements. Employers can purchase federal, state or combo posters online through any credible provider. Our trusted partner is PosterElite[13].

With the rise in the number of employees working from home many labor law poster services offer PDF or electronic versions of the federal and state posters. These can be emailed to remote employees, "posted" on the company website, or HRIS.

---

[13] https://posterelite.com/

Calculating Overtime Pay

According to the Department of Labor[14], "unless exempt, employees covered by the Act must receive overtime pay for hours worked over 40 in a workweek at a rate of not less than time and one-half their regular rate of pay."

Let's break that down:

Exempt employees are those who are exempt from minimum wage and overtime rules based on their job duties and salary. We are not talking about those employees! Non-exempt employees are those who are subject to overtime rules.

---

[14] https://www.dol.gov/agencies/whd/overtime

Federal law dictates that overtime is earned after an employee has worked more than 40 hours in a workweek. A workweek can be any fixed period of 168 hours (seven consecutive 24-hour periods). Most employers will use Monday through Sunday, Sunday through Saturday, or Saturday through Friday, but an employer could choose any day of the week to start their workweek.

A rate "not less than time and one-half" means you must pay your non-exempt employees 1.5 x's their regular rate for hours worked over 40 in any given workweek. Their regular rate is determined by calculating their gross pay and dividing it by the number of hours worked. All wages must be included in this calculation, including non-discretionary bonuses and commissions. For the full definition of regular rate of pay see the DOL's Fact Sheet #56[15].

Keep in mind states that have more favorable overtime laws take precedent over federal laws for employees working in those states.

---

[15] https://www.dol.gov/agencies/whd/
fact-sheets/56a-regular-rate

Employee Terminations

All 50 states are at-will states, which means the employer can terminate the employee at any time, with or without cause. The employer cannot terminate the employee for discriminatory reasons though, such as race, religion, or gender.

With that being said, a best practice is to have an employee handbook that outlines acceptable (and unacceptable) behavior, performance standards, attendance, etc., and to have the employee sign an acknowledgement at the time of hire.

If an employee is not performing well, the best practice is to utilize progressive discipline. This is the practice of discussing performance issues with the employee, documenting clear expectations for performance improvement, and having the employee sign each incident report. This is not required but does give the employer evidence if an employee claims a wrongful termination.

There is no federal mandate for when final wages are due, each state sets its own standards, usually differing depending on whether the employee voluntarily resigned (with or without notice), or if he or she is involuntarily terminated. California, for example, requires all wages due to the employee are paid at the time of termination.

Accrued and unused time off might be owed to the employee depending on the state the employee works in, and/or the company's internal policies.

Choosing a Pay Frequency

Each time an employer processes payroll, they must collect hours from employees, calculate the number of regular and overtime hours each employee worked, calculate the various employee taxes to withhold from employee paychecks, calculate employer taxes, pay their employees, and file and remit those taxes to the proper federal, state, or local agencies. To put it more simply, there is a large administrative burden which accompanies each payroll. These facts are important to consider when deciding how often you will pay your employees.

According to a study done by the US Bureau of Labor Statistics[16], bi-weekly payroll is the most common pay frequency used by employers, followed closely by weekly payroll, then semi-monthly and monthly.

Administratively, bi-weekly is arguably the easiest pay frequency to work with. You only run payroll ½ as often as a weekly pay cycle, but still have the benefit of a pay period which exactly matches the work week. Because the pay period aligns with the workweek, it is easy to calculate overtime.

---

[16] https://www.bls.gov/opub/btn/volume-3/how-frequently-do-private-businesses-pay-workers.htm#:~:text=Results,pay%20frequencies%20are%20less%20common.

Employers with hourly employees should opt to pay in arrears, which means the payroll is processed for a pay period that ends prior to the pay date. For example, pay on Friday for the two-week period ending on the preceding Sunday. A common example of a bi-weekly pay frequency is one which pays employees every other Friday. One downfall to this pay frequency is it does not align with accounting periods, which can add additional work for the person doing the books.

Like bi-weekly payroll, weekly payroll frequencies match the workweek schedule, making it easy to calculate and pay overtime for non-exempt employees. However, you will be processing payroll every single week, which can become a burden. There are certain industries, however, where weekly payroll is expected or considered a perk of the job, like trucking. Similar to the bi-weekly pay frequency, weekly pay frequencies will not coincide with accounting periods.

Semi-monthly pay frequencies sound easy to manage, but because the pay dates and pay period dates are based on calendar days, it can be difficult to keep track of pay period end dates, pay dates, and when payroll is due for processing. For example, if your pay dates are the 1st and the 15th, those days can vary depending on weekends and holidays (usually paid early when the pay date falls on a weekend or holiday). Unlike bi-weekly or weekly payroll where payroll is due on a certain day of the week, the payroll is due on a certain calendar day. You can be submitting payroll on any given day of the week. Semi-monthly pay frequencies also complicate first and final checks for salaried employees. Because salaried employees are paid the same amount each pay period, regardless of the number of workdays, it can be difficult to calculate prorated checks and difficult to explain the proration to employees. The upside to semi-monthly pay frequencies is the pay periods can be set up to align exactly with the accounting period.

Lastly, monthly pay frequency allows the employer to process payroll infrequently, but it is not always well-received by employees. Some states may require employers to pay employees more frequently than monthly depending on their exempt or non-exempt status.

Frequency	Pros	Cons
Weekly	Easy to calculate overtime. Benefit to employees. Acceptable in all states for all employment types. Submit payroll the same day of the week.	Lots of work. Doesn't correlate with accounting periods. Can affect monthly deductions in months where there are five checks.
Bi-Weekly	Easy to calculate overtime. Less work than weekly payroll. Acceptable in all states for all employment types. Submit payroll the same day of the week.	Doesn't correlate with accounting periods. Can affect monthly deductions in months where there are three checks.
Semi-Monthly	Coincides with accounting periods. Each month has exactly two pay dates. Easy to administer deductions.	Submission and pay days can vary depending on weekends/holidays. Can be difficult to calculate overtime.
Monthly	Least amount of work. Coincides with accounting periods.	Not all states allow all employees to be paid monthly. Employees may not like being paid only once a month. Difficult to prorate salaries.

Payroll Taxes

Payroll taxes can strike fear in the hearts of even the most seasoned payroll professionals. Payroll taxes include the taxes you withhold from employees checks as well as the employer's payroll tax liabilities. Each tax type has different deposit and filing requirements. We've created the following table to explain the major tax types, who is responsible for each tax type, and the basis for the tax calculation.

Tax Type	Employer/ Employee	Calculations
Federal Withholding	Employee	Based on wages and W-4
Social Security	Employer & Employee	6.2% paid by employee, 6.2% paid by employer, paid on wages up to the taxable wage base ($147,000 in 2022).
Medicare	Employer & Employee	1.45% paid by employee, 1.45% paid by employer, paid on ALL wages (plus an additional .9% paid by the employee for applicable wages over $200,000).
State Withholding	Employee	Based on state withholding form or federal W-4 (with the exception of states without state income tax).
Local Taxes	Employee	Local withholding rates apply
Paid Family/ Medical Leave	Depends	Each state sets its own rules for who pays the tax and what the tax rate is.
State Unemployment	Employer	Each state sets its own taxable wage base and assigns each employer their unemployment tax rate.
Federal Unemployment	Employer	6% of the first $7,000 taxable wages, with a potential credit of up to 5.4%.

Conclusion

Payroll is so much more than simple data entry, and employers should be cautious when hiring employees to ensure they follow all federal, state, and local requirements. Even employers with good intentions can end up with heavy penalties and fines if they fail to adhere to regulations. For more in-depth coverage of requirements by state, please visit us at https://valorpayrollsolutions. com/payroll-resources-for-employers/

About the Author

Christina Hageny resides in Oklahoma with her husband Rusty Hageny, an Air Force Guardsman, and her two young sons. In 2020, amid the COVID pandemic, Christina started her own independent payroll firm, Valor Payroll Solutions, which specializes in serving small and medium sized businesses. Christina not only manages payroll for her own clients, but also consults for other companies who seek her out due to her extensive knowledge in payroll.